Contents

Naming a Prehistoric Beast

All living things have a **Latin** scientific name in two parts – a **genus** name and a **species** name. You are *Homo sapiens*. A dog is *Canis familiaris* and a great white shark is *Carcharodon carcharias*. For many years scientists believed Megalodon was related to the great white shark, so it was named *Carcharodon megalodon*. Today, however, scientists think it belonged to *Carcharocles*, a genus of extinct sharks. So for now, its scientific name is *Carcharocles megalodon* – but most people just call it Megalodon!

A pod of whales is feeding on tiny plankton that floats in the warm water. As they swim to and fro they call to each other, making haunting musical sounds.

This peaceful scene is taking place in the Atlantic Ocean around three million years ago.

But a deadly threat is approaching.

Prehistoric Beasts UNCOVERED

Megalodon

The Largest Shark That Ever Lived

By Dougal Dixon

Ruby Tuesday Books

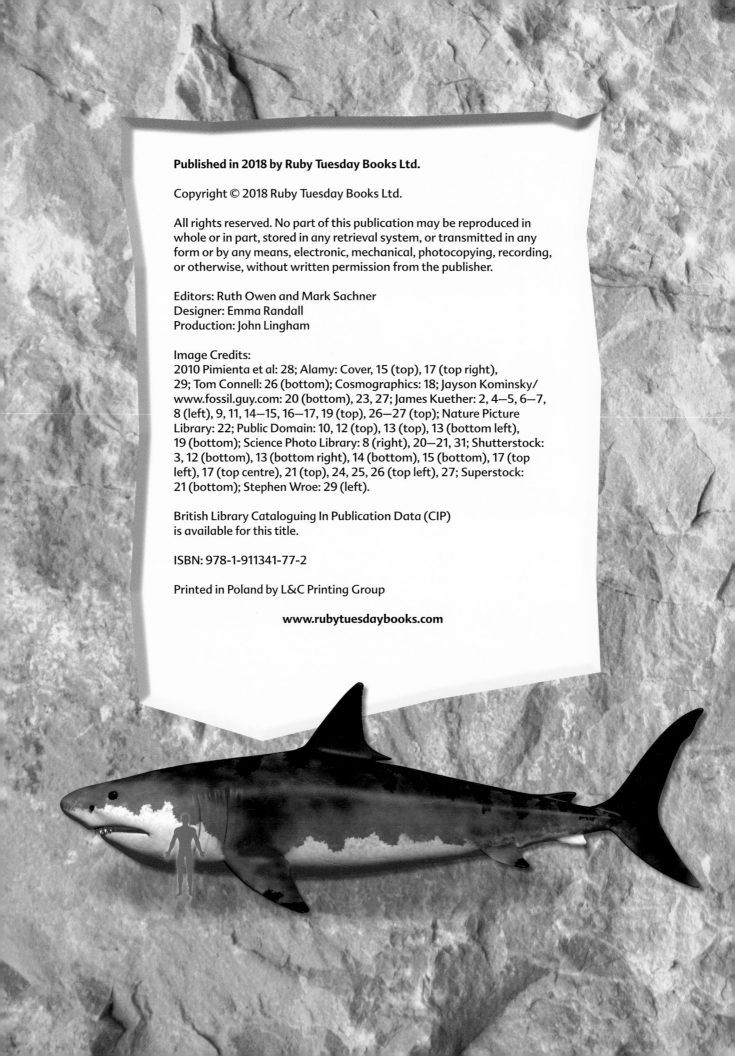

Published in 2018 by Ruby Tuesday Books Ltd.

Editors: Ruth Owen and Mark Sachner
Designer: Emma Randall
Production: John Lingham

Image Credits:
2010 Pimienta et al: 28; Alamy: Cover, 15 (top), 17 (top right), 29; Tom Connell: 26 (bottom); Cosmographics: 18; Jayson Kominsky/ www.fossil.guy.com: 20 (bottom), 23, 27; James Kuether: 2, 4—5, 6—7, 8 (left), 9, 11, 14—15, 16—17, 19 (top), 26—27 (top); Nature Picture Library: 22; Public Domain: 10, 12 (top), 13 (top), 13 (bottom left), 19 (bottom); Science Photo Library: 8 (right), 20—21, 31; Shutterstock: 3, 12 (bottom), 13 (bottom right), 14 (bottom), 15 (bottom), 17 (top left), 17 (top centre), 21 (top), 24, 25, 26 (top left), 27; Superstock: 21 (bottom); Stephen Wroe: 29 (left).

British Library Cataloguing In Publication Data (CIP) is available for this title.

ISBN: 978-1-911341-77-2

Printed in Poland by L&C Printing Group

www.rubytuesdaybooks.com

The whales have not noticed

a dark shape rising up from

the blackness below. . . .

Under Attack!

The dark shape hurtles upwards. Suddenly, the peaceful feeding scene is chaos as the whales turn and swim frantically in all directions.

No Escape

One young whale is the giant predator's target. As the great mouth sweeps by, the whale's fin is sheared off. Shocked, bleeding and unable to swim, the whale is helpless.

The Killer Blow

The attacker turns and makes its second approach. The cavernous mouth opens and the killer teeth emerge from the front of its head. It crashes into the side of the paralysed whale, tearing off flesh, crushing ribs, ripping through organs and shearing through the whale's backbone.

The attacker is a shark. And it is bigger than the whale.

This is **Megalodon** . . .
. . . the largest shark that ever lived!

Killers of the Deep

For hundreds of millions of years, the oceans have been home to fearsome hunters. These animals are the **apex predators**. They eat the other animals that share their home — but nothing eats them!

The Early Predators

Before Megalodon's deadly reign began, Earth's prehistoric oceans were home to other giant fish and swimming **reptiles**.

Armour plates instead of teeth

Dunkleosteus

Time Period: Devonian
Length: Up to 6 metres

The head and neck of *Dunkleosteus* was covered in armoured shields. Its armoured beak-like jaws were able to give a fast and powerful bite.

GEOLOGICAL TIME SCALE
To make it easier to handle prehistoric time, scientists made a time scale of the history of the Earth. It is based on how rocks form, with the oldest rocks at the bottom and the newest rocks at the top. The oldest time period is at the bottom.

Million Years Ago	Era	Time Periods
0.01	Quaternary	Holocene
2.6	Quaternary	Pleistocene
5.3	Tertiary	Pliocene
23.0	Tertiary	Miocene
33.9	Tertiary	Oligocene
55.8	Tertiary	Eocene
65.5	Tertiary	Paleocene
145.5	Mesozoic	Cretaceous
201.6	Mesozoic	Jurassic
251	Mesozoic	Triassic
299	Upper Palaeozoic	Permian
359	Upper Palaeozoic	Carboniferous
416	Upper Palaeozoic	Devonian
444	Lower Palaeozoic	Silurian
489	Lower Palaeozoic	Ordovician
542	Lower Palaeozoic	Cambrian
2500	Precambrian	Proterozoic
3800	Precambrian	Archaen
4567	Precambrian	Hadean

Cymbospondylus

Time Period: Triassic
Length: Up to 10 metres

The best known of the swimming reptiles are the ichthyosaurs. When they **evolved** from land-living reptiles, their legs became fins. Fast-swimming *Cymbospondylus* had a long snout filled with rows of teeth for grabbing fish and other prey.

Cymbospondylus

Liopleurodon

Metriorhynchus

Liopleurodon

Time Period: Jurassic
Length: Up to 6.4 metres

In the Jurassic period, the pliosaurs took over as the apex predators. *Liopleurodon* was one of the biggest pliosaurs. Its huge jaws made up about a quarter of its body length.

Mosasaurus

Time Period: Cretaceous period
Length: Up to 17 metres

In the Cretaceous period, the mosasaurs took over from the pliosaurs as the apex predators. The giant *Mosasaurus* had a long, flexible, eel-like body. It cruised the oceans feeding on fish, turtles, pterosaurs, elasmosaurs and even other mosasaurs.

Mosasaurus

The First Sharks

Sharks appeared on Earth about 400 million years ago.
At first, they came in many strange shapes.

Finding Fossils

Shark skeletons are made of **cartilage**, not bone. Cartilage is the tough, rubbery stuff that forms the outside part of your ears. When a shark dies, the cartilage usually rots away and does not **fossilise** as well as bones. This means it's very rare to find **fossils** of prehistoric sharks.

A fossilised *Helicoprion* tooth whorl

Helicoprion

Time Period: Carboniferous to Permian
Length: Estimated up to 12 metres

No one knows what *Helicoprion* looked like. The only fossilised part of the shark that's ever been found are the teeth from its lower jaw. The teeth were arranged in a curl, or whorl – like a circular saw. As new teeth grew in the jaw, they pushed the old teeth forwards to form the whorl.

The longest tooth whorl that's been found was 60 centimetres long. Scientists don't know how *Helicoprion* used its tooth whorl to eat.

Stethacanthus

Time Period: Devonian to Carboniferous
Length: 0.7 metres

Stethacanthus had an extra set of teeth mounted on its head, and another set on a fin behind its head. Scientists don't know how it used these teeth. One **theory** is that they were there to scare away predators.

Xenacanthus

Time Period: Devonian to Triassic
Length: Up to 7 metres

Xenacanthus had a long body, like a modern-day eel, and a spine that projected from the back of its head. In recent times, a new species of xenacanth has been discovered that was the size of a great white shark.

Cladoselache

Time Period: Devonian
Length: Up to 1.8 metres

Cladoselache had a rounded head, a long teardrop-shaped body, a symmetrical tail and fins on its back. It lived more than 400 million years ago, but looked a lot like a modern-day shark.

Sharks Find Their Look

At the end of the Permian period, about 251 million years ago, a catastrophic **extinction event** took place. It wiped out huge numbers of animal species, including many prehistoric sharks. The shark species that survived looked like today's modern sharks.

Permian Extinction

The cause of the Permian extinction is a mystery. It was probably connected to huge volcanic eruptions that took place in Russia. About 95 percent of ocean species were wiped out. The event is sometimes called "the great dying".

Discovering Megalodon

Around 16 million years ago, a new species of giant shark evolved. Megalodon. The biggest shark ever. The only Megalodon fossils we have are a few surviving pieces of backbone and its teeth. Thousands of enormous teeth!

Gods and Sea Monsters

Megalodon teeth have been found by archaeologists at ancient Mayan ruins in Mexico. Around 1500 years ago, the Maya people used fossil Megalodon teeth as offerings to their gods. Mayan gods and sea monsters were often drawn with just one huge tooth. This idea may have come about because the Mayans found single Megalodon teeth.

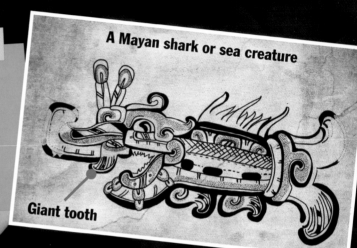

A Mayan shark or sea creature

Giant tooth

Megalodon tooth

Big Tooth

The size of Megalodon's teeth give it its name. The word Megalodon means "big tooth".

Dragon Teeth

In medieval Europe, fossilised Megalodon teeth were called "tongue stones". People thought the big, dark pointed teeth were the tongues of dragons that had been turned to stone.

A Shark from the Past

In 1667, Swedish scientist Nicolas Steno made an important discovery. Steno had examined many tongue stones. Then, one day, he was given the head of a freshly killed shark to cut up and study. Steno noticed that the shark's teeth looked very similar to tongue stones. He realised that tongue stones were the teeth of huge sharks that no longer existed.

Nicolas Steno's drawing of fossil teeth compared to a shark's head

Bashford Dean with his model Megalodon jaws at the American Museum of Natural History, in New York City

A great white shark's tooth

Big Jaws

In 1909, a scientist named Bashford Dean built a replica of Megalodon's jaws using real fossilised teeth. He based the shape of the jaws on modern-day sharks. Today, scientists think the model was the wrong shape. But it gave us a first glimpse of Megalodon.

Mega Shark

Sharks terrify and fascinate us. Therefore, it's not surprising that when we find enormous fossil shark teeth in rocks, we want to know — how did this giant creature live, what did it look like and how big did it grow?

Giant Calculations

We have found thousands of Megalodon teeth all over the world. They are the only **evidence** we have to help us calculate Megalodon's size. To do this, scientists compared the lengths of modern sharks, such as great white sharks, to the sizes of their jaws and teeth. From this they were able to estimate Megalodon's size using the dimensions of its teeth.

Dorsal fin

Megalodon
18 metres

Pectoral fin

Great White Shark
6 metres

What emerged was a whale-sized creature that was longer than a bus and could swallow a great white shark — whole! Today, most scientists agree that Megalodon could grow to a length of up to 18 metres.

A shark's mouth is like a conveyor belt of teeth. As the front teeth fall out, new ones are waiting to move forward.

20,000 Teeth

Sharks continuously replace their teeth as they grow and wear out. A single shark can generate and lose 20,000 teeth in its life. It's safe to assume that this was the same for Megalodon, and explains why we have found so many fossilised teeth.

Great white shark

Rows of teeth

Second dorsal fin

Caudal fin

Anal fin

Megalodon Stats

Scientists have estimated these statistics based on an 18-metre-long adult Megalodon.

Weight: About 50 tonnes
Height of dorsal fin: 1.9 metres
Length of pectoral fin: 3.6 metres
Pectoral fins tip to tip: 10 metres
Caudal (tail fin) tip to tip: 4.5 metres

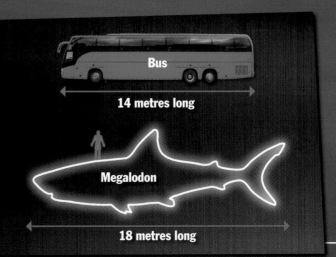

Bus

14 metres long

Megalodon

18 metres long

A Killing Machine

We all know what a shark looks like. A **streamlined**, teardrop-shaped body. A mouthful of sharp teeth and a tall triangular dorsal fin cutting through the water — in fact, the perfect, high-speed, aquatic killing machine. We are pretty sure that Megalodon fitted this picture.

What Did Megalodon Look Like?

For now, we don't know how closely Megalodon is related to modern sharks. But by looking at its teeth, scientists think it probably looked a lot like a great white shark.

Like Jaws, But Bigger!

To support its enormous teeth Megalodon would have needed stronger jaw bones than a great white. Its shoulder area would also have been more massive to support the jaws. Scientists also think it had a more domed head and a shorter snout.

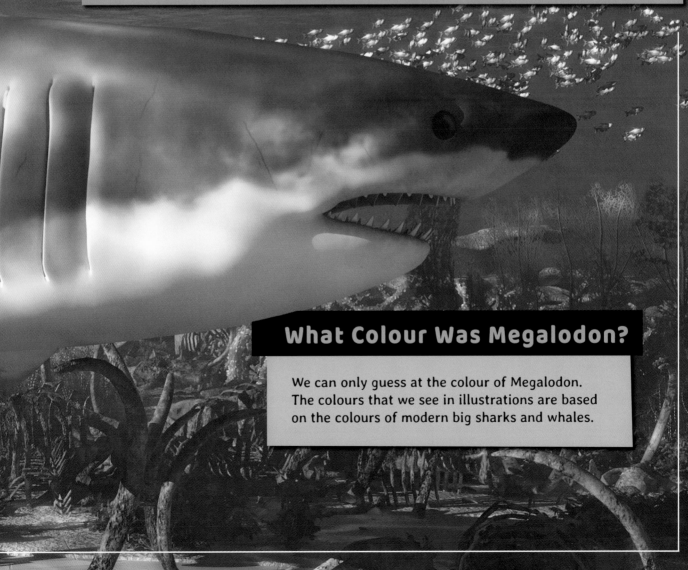

Could Scientists Be Wrong?

We think that Megalodon looked like a big great white shark because the teeth of the two animals are so similar. However, an effect called convergence could mean we've all got it wrong! Convergence says that a feature, such as teeth, can evolve to look the same in two different animals because the teeth do the same job. However, the rest of the animal might look very different.

Megalodon tooth

Great white shark tooth

Lion's eye

Elephant's eye

For example, a lion's eyeball and an elephant's eyeball do the same job so they look similar. However, the rest of each animal is very different from the other. Maybe Megalodon actually looked nothing like the sharks we know today!

What Colour Was Megalodon?

We can only guess at the colour of Megalodon. The colours that we see in illustrations are based on the colours of modern big sharks and whales.

Megalodon's World

The fossilised teeth of Megalodon have been found throughout the world.

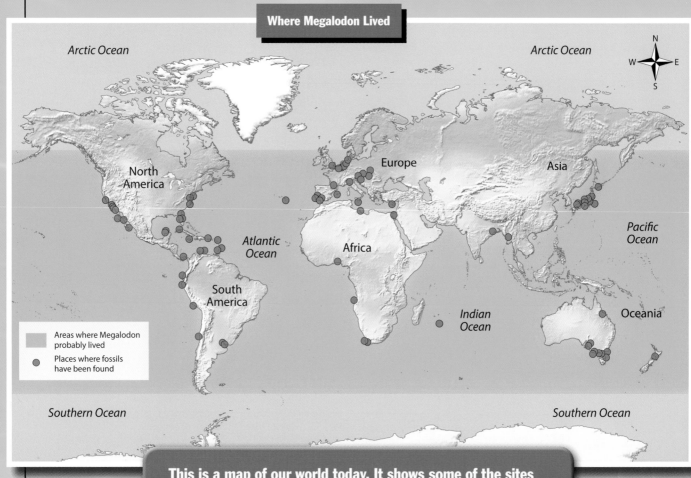

Where Megalodon Lived

Arctic Ocean

Arctic Ocean

North America

Europe

Asia

Atlantic Ocean

Africa

Pacific Ocean

South America

Indian Ocean

Oceania

Southern Ocean

Southern Ocean

Areas where Megalodon probably lived

Places where fossils have been found

This is a map of our world today. It shows some of the sites where Megalodon fossils have been found. The fossil finds tell scientists that Megalodon lived in most of Earth's oceans in areas where the waters were warm.

Fossil Hunting

Fossil hunters have discovered Megalodon teeth on beaches and projecting out of rocky cliffs. They have been found far from the sea in deserts and even on mountains. This is because, millions of years ago, these places were covered by oceans.

Did Meg Meet Jaws?

It's possible that Megalodon and the great white shark were ocean neighbours. Some scientists think the great white evolved around 16 million years ago. This means the two predators lived and hunted in the same prehistoric oceans.

Megalodon's Habitats

As an adult, Megalodon lived in all sorts of ocean habitats. It seems to have moved from coastal waters into deep oceans and into shallow lagoons. Scientists can't say for sure, but it may have lived in different places at different stages of its life, hunting different prey.

Did Megalodon and *Livyatan* ever do battle? For now, no evidence has been found.

Livyatan

Megalodon

Livyatan

Megalodon shared its role of apex predator with prehistoric whales, including the mighty *Livyatan*. This extinct sperm whale was the same size as Megalodon and had the largest teeth of any animal that ever lived. Megalodon and *Livyatan* may have competed for food. They may even have fed on each other's young!

A replica of a *Livyatan* skull and teeth.

Livyatan's teeth grew to more than 30 centimetres long!

Mega Meat-Eater

By the time Megalodon appeared, 16 million years ago, Earth's oceans were home to mammals such as whales, manatees, seals and sea lions. All these animals would have been hunted and killed by Megalodon.

A Perfect Kill

When attacking a whale, Megalodon first tore off the animal's fins. Then, with its victim bleeding and unable to swim away, the great shark went in for the kill. Its jaws broke through the ribcage to get at the whale's heart, lungs and other vital organs.

A Back-Breaking Bite

There is fossil evidence that Megalodon killed whales. A fossilised section of a whale's **vertebra** shows that the whale's backbone was bitten in half by the shark. It's possible to see gashes in the bone that match Megalodon's saw-like teeth.

Fossilised whale bone

Gashes from a Megalodon's tooth

Time to Enjoy a Meal

Most of a modern shark's muscles are used for great bursts of speed. However, the shark quickly gets tired. If Megalodon crippled its giant prey first, it was then able to kill and eat its meal without any rush or panic.

Killer Teeth

The biggest Megalodon teeth that have been found are 18 centimetres long. Each tooth is edged with hundreds of razor-sharp points called serrations.

Not a Fussy Eater!

Sharks are what we call opportunistic feeders. This means they feed on anything they get the opportunity to eat. Scientists think that Megalodon may have fed on big fish, turtles and other sharks. Perhaps they even **scavenged** the bodies of large land animals that were washed out to sea by floods!

Scenting Blood

Sharks can scent blood and prey in seawater many kilometres away. They can detect chemicals called necromones that are released by dead bodies. It's likely that Megalodon could do this, too.

Megalodon's Life Story

A Megalodon began its life in a warm, shallow area of water close to the coast. This is called a nursery area.

Shark Nursery Areas

Modern sharks give birth to their pups in nursery areas. These are places where there is plenty of food. Nurseries are also safer for young animals because the water is too shallow for some large predators to swim there. Shark pups live in nursery areas until they are big enough to head out into the open oceans.

Megalodon Mums and Pups

Unlike other fish that lay eggs, most modern sharks give birth to live young. Scientists think it's likely that Megalodon did the same.

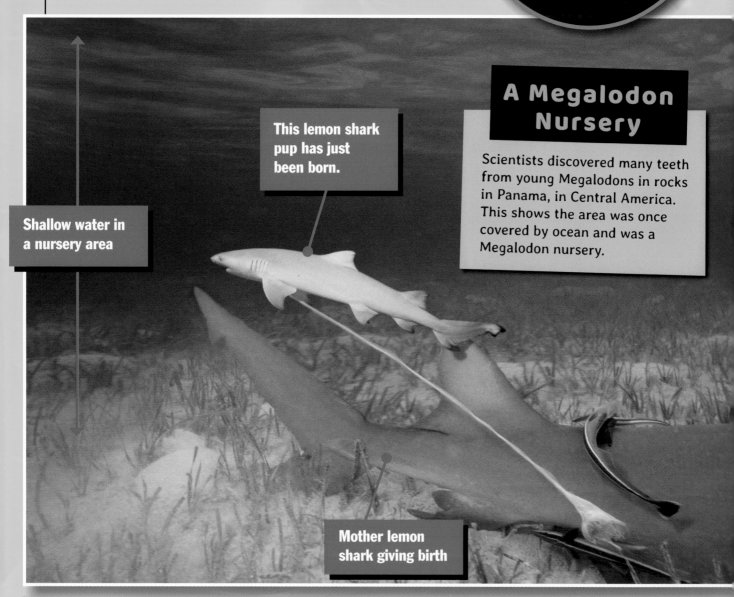

This lemon shark pup has just been born.

Shallow water in a nursery area

A Megalodon Nursery

Scientists discovered many teeth from young Megalodons in rocks in Panama, in Central America. This shows the area was once covered by ocean and was a Megalodon nursery.

Mother lemon shark giving birth

y Food

ng Megalodons probably ate fish, dolphins,
ongs and turtles. Once they grew up and left
nursery areas, they hunted big whales.

Bone Crunchers

The biggest Megalodon teeth, from older animals,
often show fractures at the tips. This damage was
caused by constant pressure against something
extremely hard, like bone. Some scientists think this
could mean that elderly Megalodons were mainly
scavengers. They would have fed on the corpses of
dead whales, crunching into their bones after younger
animals had eaten most of the soft meat.

**Broken tip
of tooth**

ing represents
of growth.

**Shark
vertebrae**

More Than
It Could Chew

Scientists have discovered a
4-million-year-old whale rib that has three
tooth marks from a Megalodon. New bone had
grown to heal the wounds, which shows the whal
escaped and survived the attack. By measuring
the distance between the tooth marks, scientist
estimated the Megalodon was between 4
and 7 metres long. The shark was only
a youngster, but it was capable of
attacking an adult whale much
bigger than itself!

Growth Rings

Sometimes fossilised Megalodon vertebrae, or backbones, are
discovered. Like the rest of the skeleton, these were made of
cartilage. However, they also contained **calcium** that made them
harder and more likely to fossilise. Shark vertebrae have growth
rings like the rings that form in tree trunks. The growth rings in
some Megalodon vertebrae show the animals were 25 to 40 years old.
It is likely that Megalodon could live to be older than this.

Extinction of Megalodon

Megalodon was the terror of the oceans for around 14 million years. Then, it became extinct. Why?

A Mass-Extinction Event

Around 2.6 million years ago, the **ice age** began. At this time, ocean currents changed and many shallow seas were lost as ocean levels dropped. This caused a mass-extinction event in the world's oceans.

Losing Megalodon

More than 50 percent of whale species died out and about 9 percent of shark species were lost — including Megalodon. Did these changes in the oceans and Earth's climate lead to Megalodon's extinction? Perhaps the loss of so many prey animals made it impossible for a large predator like Megalodon to survive.

Today, the largest predatory shark alive is the great white. Megalodon is gone forever.

Could Megalodon Still Be Alive?

It's an exciting thought, but science says no! In order for Megalodon to be alive, it would have to breed. To do this, there would need to be a large number of these animals in the ocean and there have been no sightings. Also, no Megalodon bodies or fresh, unfossilised teeth have ever been found.

An Ocean Success Story

Sharks were living on Earth before the dinosaurs. Over time there have been thousands of different species. The dinosaurs, the great swimming reptiles and many other prehistoric animals are gone. But sharks have survived. Today, there are more than 400 different shark species in Earth's oceans.

How Did Megalodon's Teeth Become Fossils?

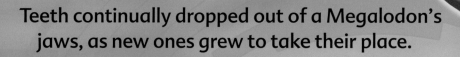

Teeth continually dropped out of a Megalodon's jaws, as new ones grew to take their place.

A Megalodon tooth was made up of different layers:
- Soft pulp in the middle surrounded by dentine.
- An outside skin of hard enamel.

4 Million Years Ago

A tooth settles on the seabed. Layers of **sediment** build up on top of the tooth. After 15,000 years the pulp and dentine rot. These materials are replaced by **minerals** from water and the surrounding sediments.

After 100,000 years, the inside of the tooth has been completely replaced by minerals. It has become a fossil.

2 Million Years Ago

The ocean has dried up. The layers of sediment have been crushed and cemented together, forming rock.

Movements in the Earth's crust push the rock upward, forming mountains above the fossil.

Wind, rain and snow begin to wear the mountains down.

Today

As the rocks around the fossil tooth are **eroded**, it becomes exposed. One day it is found by a fossil hunter.

When Did Megalodon Go Extinct?

In 2014, a team of scientists in Florida and Switzerland set out to answer this question. They decided to use fossil teeth to calculate when Megalodon died out.

Studying Fossils

It's possible to work out approximately how long ago a layer of rock formed. If a fossil tooth is found in that rock, its age will be similar. The **research** team studied more than 50 fossil teeth from rocks that had formed in the past few million years. The ages of the teeth could be estimated from the age of the rocks where they were discovered. The scientists found that all of the teeth were older than 2.6 million years old.

Why Are Megalodon's Teeth Black?

Just like your teeth, a living shark's teeth are white. So why are fossil teeth sometimes black or other colours? The fossil teeth are made of minerals, just like the rocks where the fossils formed. It's the minerals that give the teeth their colours.

A fossil Megalodon tooth embedded in rock

Megalodon Disappears

The team's work showed there had been no Megalodon teeth around to become fossils for about 2.6 million years. This confirmed that Megalodon probably became extinct around that time.

Millions of years ago these Megalodon teeth were white.

A Megalodon Nursery and Killer Bites

In 2010, a group of scientists led by Megalodon expert Catalina Pimiento announced they had discovered a Megalodon nursery. The team made their discovery in Panama, in Central America.

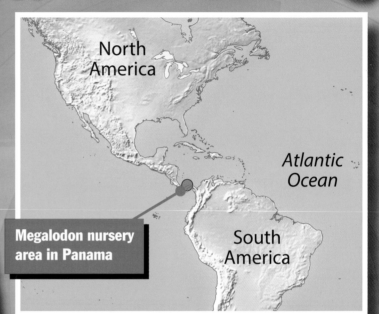

North America

Atlantic Ocean

Megalodon nursery area in Panama

South America

These teeth from the Panama site are life-size.

Tooth Collecting

The team collected fossil Megalodon teeth from rocky areas that were once part of a shallow sea. They measured the Megalodon teeth and compared them to teeth from other areas. All the teeth were small. But were they just the smaller teeth that grew at the sides of an adult Megalodon's jaws?

The Evidence Proves It

At other Megalodon fossil sites, scientists had found small teeth mixed in with larger ones. In Panama, the team found hardly any large teeth. The data showed that all the teeth came from Megalodon pups. This proved the area was a nursery. Catalina and her team had found a place where Megalodons went to give birth – more than 10 million years ago!

How Long Was a Baby Megalodon?

By measuring the teeth the team were able to estimate the sizes of the baby sharks. They ranged from 2 metres long to 10.5 metres. The 2-metre-long pups were probably newborns.

Newborn Megalodon

How Hard Could Megalodon Bite?

Measuring Bite Force

Scientist Stephen Wroe wanted to answer this question. To test Megalodon's bite he used the same technology that engineers use when designing cars, bridges or even spacecraft. Stephen took **CT scans** of a great white shark's skull. These X-ray images were used to create a 3D computer model of the shark's skull and jaws. Next, Stephen used a technique called finite element analysis to work out the strength of the skull. This is shown on a computer with different parts and different properties being shown in different colours. The computer model was then put through lots of tests to calculate the force of a great white shark's bite.

A shark skull created using finite element analysis.

Back-Breaking Bite Force

Once Stephen knew the bite force of a great white, he was able to scale up this information for a shark the size of Megalodon. The data showed that Megalodon's jaws could generate about 18,000 kilograms of force. Its bite was like the weight of ten SUVs crushing down onto its prey. More than enough to snap the backbone of a whale!

Glossary

apex predator
An animal at the top of a food chain. An apex predator eats other animals in its habitat but is too big or powerful to be killed and eaten itself.

calcium
An element that is important in the structure of bones and eggshells.

cartilage
A tough, flexible material in the bodies of animals. For example, cartilage forms the outer part of a person's ears.

CT scan
A highly detailed X-ray picture that is taken by a computed tomography (CT) scanner. A CT scanner takes a series of cross-section photographs of a person or animal's body.

erode
To wear away a rock or landscape. Weather, rivers, landslides and even walking animals all cause erosion.

evidence
Information that can be used to show that something is true. For example, Megalodon tooth marks in whale bones are evidence that the shark ate whales.

evolve
To change or develop slowly, often over a long period of time.

extinction event
When a number of different groups of animals die out at the same time for the same cause.

fossil
The hard remains of a living thing that are preserved in rock.

fossilise
To become a fossil.

genus
A classification of living things. A genus may cover several species. For example, the genus *Panthera* includes *Panthera leo*, the lion, and *Panthera tigris*, the tiger.

ice age
A period of the Earth's history when climates are much cooler than usual and ice caps and glaciers expand. The last ice age started 2.6 million years ago and only finished about 10,000 years ago.

Latin
A language that began in ancient Rome. Scientists still use Latin today when naming animals, plants and other living things.

mineral
A solid material that is formed by natural processes and is found in soil or water. Rocks are made of minerals.

reptile
One of a group of backboned animals that are cold-blooded and usually lay eggs on land. Lizards, snakes, crocodiles and turtles are reptiles.

research
Information that is gathered and studied in order to prove facts.

scavenge
To feed on dead plants or the bodies of dead animals.

sediment
Particles of sand or mud that have accumulated at the bottom of a river, lake or ocean.

species
Different types of living things. The members of an animal species look alike and can produce young together.

streamlined
Having a smooth shape that cuts down on resistance when moving through water or air.

theory
An idea or belief that is based on limited information. A theory can be proved with evidence.

vertebra
One of the bones (or vertebrae) that form the spine, or backbone.

Index

Learn More Online
Could you be a scientist uncovering the buried secrets of prehistoric beasts?
Go to: www.rubytuesdaybooks.com/dinosaurs